THE PRAYING ATHLETE
QUOTE BOOK

VOL 2

TEAM WORK

Published by The Core Media Group, Inc., P.O. Box 2037, Indian Trail, NC 28079.

Cover & Interior Design: Ashlyn Helms

Printed in the United States of America.

VOL 2 TEAM WORK

Be the teammate you seek in your peers, and you will build a better team.

"Each of you should use whatever gift you have received to serve others, as faithful stewards of God's grace in its various forms."
1 Peter 4:10

You can prolong your career by putting the right people on your team.

"As iron sharpens iron, so one person sharpens another."
Proverbs 27:17

To be aligned with your team means you must be totally committed to what is best for your team, not yourself.

"Do to others as you would have them do to you."
Luke 6:31

Pleasing your coach cannot be your focus. The purpose of the team should be your focus.

"For even the Son of Man did not come to be served, but to serve, and to give his life as a ransom for many."
Mark 10:45

**Every team is under
construction daily.
Be patient.**

"But if we hope for what we do not yet
have, we wait for it patiently."
Romans 8:25

**Encourage your teammates,
and you will be encouraged.**

"Do not let any unwholesome talk
come out of your mouths, but only what
is helpful for building others up
according to their needs, that it may
benefit those who listen."
Ephesians 4:29

**Toss out all your team's
emotional garbage
and start fresh today.**

"But now, by dying to what once bound
us, we have been released from the law
so that we serve in the new
way of the Spirit, and not in the
old way of the written code."
Romans 7:6

**Live through the struggles and
victories with your teammates—
teamwork is a journey
of endurance.**

"From him the whole body, joined and
held together by every supporting
ligament, grows and builds itself up in
love, as each part does its work."
Ephesians 4:16

**The discipline of being a good
team member is real work.**

"Not looking to your own interests
but each of you to the interest
of the others."
Philippians 2:4

**Saying to a teammate,
"Let me help you," can go
a long way in building
an unbreakable bond.**

"And do not forget to do good and to
share with others, for with such
sacrifices God is pleased."
Hebrews 13:16

**Acknowledging those who help
you makes others want to help
you and your team.**

"We always thank God for all of you
and continually mention you
in our prayers."
1 Thessalonians 1:2

**Forgiveness opens new doors
in team relationships.**

"Be kind and compassionate to one
another, forgiving each other, just as in
Christ God forgave you."
Ephesians 4:32

**Find two things you like
about a team and
let the teammates know.
This will build unity and trust.**

"Finally, brothers and sisters, rejoice!
Strive for full restoration, encourage
one another, be of one mind, live
in peace. And the God of love and
peace will be with you."
2 Corinthians 13:11

Be thankful that you are part of a team. You are part of something greater than yourself.

"Let the peace of Christ rule in your hearts, since as members of one body you were called to peace.
And be thankful."
Colossians 3:15

**Whether you like your team
or not, embrace
each other's differences.**

"There are different kinds of gifts, but
the same Spirit distributes them. There
are different kinds of service, but the
same Lord. There are different kinds of
working but in all of them and in everyone it is the same God at work."
1 Corinthians 12:4-6

Say, "I'm committed to help build this team." Once voiced, it can come alive in your spirit, and the team can flourish.

"For the word of God is alive and active. Sharper than any double-edged sword, it penetrates even to the dividing soul and spirit, joints and marrow; it judges the thoughts and attitudes of the heart."
Hebrews 4:12

**A good team will always say it
loved its coach and each other.
Breathe the right love language
into your team.**

"Above all, love each other
deeply, because love covers over a
multitude of sins."
1 Peter 4:8

Do not allow your teammates to turn you into a puppet. Instead, enable your teammates to show you how to grow, and hold on to your own identity.

"In fact, though by this time you ought to be teachers, you need someone to teach you the elementary truths of God's word all over again. You need milk, not solid food! Anyone who lives on milk, being still an infant, is not acquainted with the teaching about righteousness."
Hebrews 5:12-13

Build your team within your community. Serve together, walk together, laugh together, love each other, and together you will be forever remembered as a team that accomplished much. A team can bring hope to a community.

"Therefore, as God's chosen people, holy and dearly loved, clothe yourselves with compassion, kindness, humility, gentleness and patience. Bear with each other and forgive one another if any of you has a grievance against someone. Forgive as the Lord forgave you. And over all these virtues put on love, which binds them all together in perfect unity."
Colossians 3:12-14

If teammates and coaches focus on your bad traits, chances are you will be discouraged. However, you can focus on the good traits of your teammates and coaches. By encouraging one another, each person grows as a player and teammate.

"I myself am convinced, my brothers and sisters, that you yourselves are full of goodness, filled with knowledge and competent to instruct one another."
Romans 15:14

**Rise to the occasion as a unit,
instead of as an individual.**

"Let us therefore make every effort to
do what leads to peace
and to mutual edification."
Romans 14:19

**Championships are for teams
who listen to the same voice.**

"Turning your ear to wisdom and
applying your heart to understanding."
Proverbs 2:2

**You cannot choose
your teammates, but you can
change their attitudes with
encouragement and support.**

"Now that you have purified yourselves
by obeying the truth so that you have
sincere love for each other, love one
another deeply, from the heart."
1 Peter 1:22

**To be a winner, surround yourself
with winners.**

"Walk with the wise and become wise,
for a companion of fools suffers harm."
Proverbs 13:20

Teach your team to play with the passion that fuels you.

"Then make my joy complete by being like-minded, having the same love, being one in spirit and of one mind."
Philippians 2:2

Maintain your value as a teammate by being present, diligent, and enduring the process, no matter the circumstance.

"Do your best to present yourself to God as one approved, a worker who does not need to be ashamed and who correctly handles the word of truth."
2 Timothy 2:15

Listen to the voices of your teammates. They might have something to teach you.

"Listen to advice and accept discipline, and at the end you will be counted among the wise."
Proverbs 19:20

What value can you bring to the team besides your physical skills?

"For physical training is of some value, but godliness has value for all things, holding promise for both the present life and the life to come."
1 Timothy 4:8

**Would you want your teammates
to play with your passion
and energy?**

"Being strengthened with all power
according to his glorious might so that
you may have great endurance
and patience..."
Colossians 1:11

Teams need more troubleshooters and fewer troublemakers. The troubleshooters find ways to shut down the troublemakers, making room for unity and team chemistry. Be a troubleshooter!

"I appeal to you, brothers and sisters, in the name of our Lord Jesus Christ, that all of you agree with one another in what you say and that there be no divisions among you, but that you be perfectly united in mind and thought."
1 Corinthians 1:10

THOUGHTS & REFLECTIONS

_____

_____

_____

_____

_____

_____

_____

_____

_____

_____

_____

_____

_____

_____

_____

_____

_____

_____

_____

_____

_____

_____

_____

_____

_____

_____

_____

_____

_____

_____

_____

_____

_____

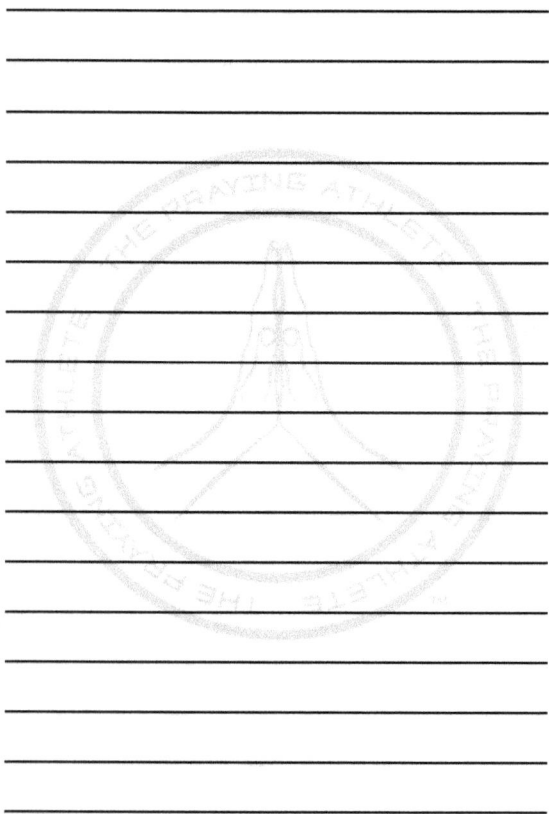

_____

_____

_____

_____

_____

_____

_____

_____

_____

_____

_____

_____

_____

_____

_____

_____

_____

_____

_____

_____

_____

_____

_____

_____

_____

_____

_____

_____

_____

_____

_____

_____

MY QUOTES

_____

_____

_____

_____

_____

_____

_____

_____

_____

_____

_____

_____

_____

_____

_____

_____

_____

_____

_____

_____

_____

_____

_____

_____

_____

_____

_____

_____

_____

_____

ACKNOWLEDGEMENTS

I want to acknowledge and say thank you to all those that helped with this project:

Nadia Guy
Ashlyn Helms
My Mom & Dad

All of my NFL Clients, current and former, that have encouraged me to share these words with others.

ABOUT
TPA

The Praying Athlete is a movement that creates an organic culture of prayer through an uplifting community and authentic conversation.

For more information, visit our website **www.theprayingathlete.com**.

Follow us on social media.

 @ThePrayingAthlete

 @Praying_Athlete

 @ThePrayingAthlete

COLLECT ALL
8 VOL.

Our first volume of *The Praying Athlete Quote Book* addresses the topic of playing the game. Quotes and thoughts from Robert B. Walker, paired with Scripture from God's Word, allow readers to get a good idea about what playing a good game looks like.

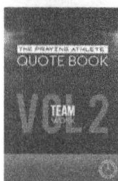

Our second volume of *The Praying Athlete Quote Book* addresses the topic of teamwork. Quotes and thoughts from Robert B. Walker, paired with Scripture from God's Word, allow readers to understand what it means to be a good teammate and surround yourself with people who lift you up.

Our third volume of *The Praying Athlete Quote Book* addresses the topic of growth & preparation for the future. Quotes and thoughts from Robert B. Walker, paired with Scripture from God's Word, allow readers to know that even though the future is uncertain, there is a plan and purpose for everyone.

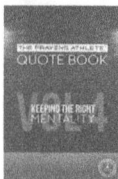

Our fourth volume of *The Praying Athlete Quote Book* addresses the topic of keeping the right mentality. Quotes and thoughts from Robert B. Walker allow readers to understand how staying in the right mindset can improve overall performance.

Our fifth volume of *The Praying Athlete Quote Book* addresses the topic of staying motivated. Quotes and thoughts from Robert B. Walker allow readers to become motivated to accomplish their goals, even when they feel they are not up to the task.

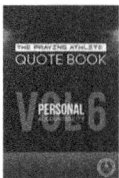

Our sixth volume of *The Praying Athlete Quote Book* addresses the topic of personal accountability. Quotes and thoughts from Robert B. Walker allow readers to think about how they can better themselves. Whether its ending a bad habit or saying no to anything that may hurt themselves or others, staying accountable will benefit one's character and performance.

Our seventh volume of *The Praying Athlete Quote Book* addresses the topic of living life. This volume is the first part in a two part living life series. Quotes and thoughts from Robert B. Walker give readers a better understanding of how to live life to the fullest.

Our eighth volume of *The Praying Athlete Quote Book* addresses the topic of living life. This volume is the second part in a two part living life series. Quotes and thoughts from Robert B. Walker give readers a better understanding of how to live life to the fullest.

FOR MORE INFO AND MERCHANDISE, PLEASE VISIT WWW.THEPRAYINGATHLETE.COM

CHECK OUT OUR

THE PRAYING ATHLETE™
PHOTOGRAPHY
QUOTE BOOKS

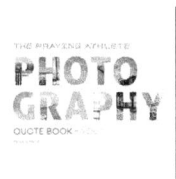

VOL. 1

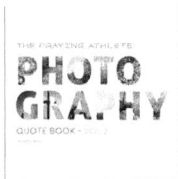

VOL. 2

VOL. 3

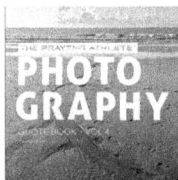

VOL. 4

*The Praying Athlete Photography Quote Book*s celebrate God's glory and magnificence through His creation. They contain photos taken by Robert B. Walker, paired with his words of wisdom, motivation, and inspiration.

www.ingramcontent.com/pod-product-compliance
Lightning Source LLC
Chambersburg PA
CBHW071745020426
42331CB00008B/2193